Charles M Scott

The Origin of the Tennessee Campaign

Charles M Scott

The Origin of the Tennessee Campaign

ISBN/EAN: 9783742809698

Manufactured in Europe, USA, Canada, Australia, Japa

Cover: Foto ©ninafisch / pixelio.de

Manufactured and distributed by brebook publishing software
(www.brebook.com)

Charles M Scott

The Origin of the Tennessee Campaign

THE ORIGIN

TENNESSEE -:- CAMPAIGN,

By CAPT. CHARLES M. SCOTT,

AS A REFUTATION OF

THE FRADULENT CLAIM OF MISS ANNA ELLA CARROLL.

TERRE HAUTE, IND. :
MOORE & LANGEN, PRINTERS AND BINDERS.
1885.

Introduction and Explanation.

*To the Citizens of the United States, and the Senators and
Members of the House of Representatives in particular:*

The author of these papers having become aware that another
attempt is about to be made during the next meeting of Congress
to renew the fraudulent claim of Miss Carroll for compensation
for furnishing the information to the War Department that led
to the movement up the Tennessee River in the Spring of 1862;
and as it is clear to all that this movement was the turning
point of the war, four different efforts have been made to carry
such a claim through Congress, each more determined than
the last, and as I am getting old and cannot expect to live many
years, being now in my seventy-fifth year, I deem it my duty
to prevent this raid on the Treasury that I am sure is being
prepared for during the present administration.   And by re-
publishing the same evidence that I laid before the Committee
on Military affairs, to whom it was referred August 8, 1876,
and printed in Miscellaneous Document No. 179, of the House
of Representatives of the first session of the Forty-fourth Congress.

The following is the evidence I furnished and which was
printed in aforesaid pamphlet, beginning at Page 16 and extend-
ing to Page 27, and consists mainly of her own publications
and letters from others, and altogether such a mass of proof
as must forever destroy such a fraudulent claim if properly
spread before the public.

I also deem it proper to solve the enigma of how Grant secured the command of the advance up the Tennessee River. after what the public deemed his defeat at Belmont. Also the cause of the difficulty between Grant and Halleck and again the warm feeling between Grant and Washburn. And as they are all only different parts of the same problem, and which is alluded to in the letters of both Major Gillam and John Barclay in their allusion to my having taken Miss Carroll's letter to Grant to read.

The simple facts are that knowing all the facts in relation to the Belmont affair, and that instead of being, as the world esteemed it, a failure, it was the best planned and best executed of any piece of strategy during the war, and its moral effect was greater in proportion than any event that occurred during the war, and as the public was unjust in its judgments in considering it a defeat, inasmuch as we did not hold the ground, they not knowing why it was fought claimed it as a defeat, I thought that if I gave him the information in my possession it might lead to his advancement to the command of the expedition.

Hence in conversation with my friends Major Gillam and Mr. Barclay, I asked them what they thought about showing Grant the letters. Both of them warmly approved of the idea, and that same evening after 5:00 P. M., December the 15th, 1861, I took the copy of my first paper sent to the Secretary of War, directed to the care of Miss Carroll, and then her answer ; then a copy of my second letter, and then her letter, informing me that my information had been found to be correct.

When I told Grant that I had some papers to show him he said, "Wait a little, I will soon be through."

In a short time he took me to his private office, where I handed him first, a copy of my first letter to the War Department, and directed to the care of Miss Carroll; then her reply; third, my second letter, and lastly the announcement of the fact that they found my statements correct and that the movement up the Tennessee was resolved on. When he got through reading them he straightened up and drawing one or two whiffs from a cigar that had been out half an hour, said. "Well, Scott, I know nothing about this, what do you want me to do about it?" I told him that all I ever aspired to be was a first-class pilot and I knew I was that, but that he, as a military man, man, seeing what was going to be done by making a proper application, might get command of the expedition and add a feather to his cap or a star to his shoulder. He then rang a bell and sent for Colonel Rawlins, and when Rawlins took his seat Grant handed him the papers in the same rotation that I had handed them to him (Grant). When Rawlins got through them he said: "There is something in this, General," and pushing the papers back to Grant reached over and drew to him a block of foolscap, and whilst Grant asked questions from the papers Rawlins wrote down my answers. The questions asked were for the purpose of explanation and drawing out such other facts as made the whole thing much clearer.

After the whole was written out the question arose what use was to be made of it?

According to military etiquette it was Grant's duty to have forwarded it to his superior officer, General Halleck, at St. Louis. But Rawlins urged him not to do so, but to send it to Washburn, at Washington, and I seconded his opinion. And whatever might have occurred before I am very certain that Halleck had just ground of complaint against Grant, for the next day I walked with Rawlins to the postoffice and saw him mail a letter to Mr. Washburn, and I am very certain that it was Washburn's influence that secured Grant's reinstatement after Halleck had retired him at Pittsburg Landing.

The following is taken from Miscellaneous Document No. 179, of the House of Representatives of the Forty-fourth Congress, and on file in the Library of Congress, beginning at Page 16 and continued to and including Page 27.

" Charles M. Scott being duly sworn, made the following statement:

" At the beginning of the war I had to leave New Orleans. I left on the night of the last of May, 1861, ran away, you may say. I came up to Memphis, and there I was stopped by Gideon J. Pillow, who commanded there, and seized my boat to use her in the Confederate service. I had a quarter interest in the boat. Pillow gave a certificate of valuation for the boat, to be paid when we proved our allegiance to the Confederate Government. I asked him for a pass to St. Louis. He refused unless I would take oath of allegiance to the Confederate Government. I afterwards escaped from Memphis and started for Cairo, and whilst the boat I was on was lying at New Madrid, I got information that the Confederate authorities had missed me and telegraphed ahead of me to Columbus and that it was dangerous to go there, so I got off and went by land to Cairo. I got into Cairo about the 19th of June, 1861. I went to General Prentice and reported myself to him, and he finding that I was a pilot and having seen the fortifications reported to be there he asked me to make a drawing of them and a sketch of the river in that vicinity. I made a sketch of the batteries and also the Mississippi River from Norfolk, twenty miles below, to Ashport, one hundred miles above Memphis. After that he having no further use for me at the time, he took my address in Ohio (as I intended to take my wife there and leave her with her relations) I left for St. Louis and from there to Ohio.

The day the news reached Columbus, Ohio, that General Grant was appointed I came right back to Cairo. I reported to admiral Foot on the way, he had no use for me at the time. I went on to Cairo and was appointed to the transport Belle

Memphis, Grant's headquarters boat. During the time I lay
at Cairo I had frequent conversations with one or two men
that I knew to be loyal. There were so many disloyal that I
was afraid to trust anybody, and I then matured in my mind
a campaign on the Tennessee River. I knew the country as a
boy. This was in the latter part of September I reported to
Grant as a pilot ready for duty. I had this plan but had no
means of making it known. I was almost afraid to let my
right hand know what my left was doing because I considered
that every one I knew was a traitor and there were only one or
two I could trust even in the Army. I looked on half of them
as rebels. However, in conversation with one of the men I .
have mentioned, Major Barclay C. Gillam (belonging to the
28th Regiment Illinois Volunteers) and lived in Rushville,
Illinois, I often discussed the Tennessee campaign.

At the battle of Belmont I had a front seat and when the
ball was over and we got back to Cairo, when I lay down to
rest I became so infernally scared I could neither sleep, stand
up or lay down at the time. I wrote a letter to my wife the
next day, and she received it on Sunday at 2 o'clock, as she
came down to dinner, so I have heard her say. This is how
we came to the intercourse with Miss Carroll. My wife was
stopping at the Everett House in St. Louis. When my wife
returned to the dinner table and Mrs. Merrit (the landlady)
asked her if that letter was from her husband and she answered,
yes. Mrs. Merritt then asked her if it spoke of the battle of
Belmont. She answered, yes, it told all about it. Several ladies
at the table requested Mrs. Merrit to ask my wife to allow them to
hear such parts of the letter read as related to the battle, the most
of them having friends in the Army. My wife invited them
to her room and read it to them. Among those who heard the
letter read was Miss Anna Ella Carroll. She reported it to
Evans and he requested to be allowed to read the letter. He
read the letter and then he expressed a desire to know who I
was, and Mr. Merrit, landlord of the hotel (who knew me well)

gave him my history. When I arrived in St. Louis on the Saturday following (I came up with the Fifth Iowa to go to Benton Barracks) I received a note signed Judge Evans, of Texas, asking me to call at the Everett House (my wife had left the hotel and went to keeping house) I sent word that I would call on Sunday as I had been up all night and was both tired and sleepy. I have not preserved that note, I did not think it of sufficient importance. However, I called and found Judge Evans and Miss Carroll there, and in conversation about the battle of Belmont. One word led to another and Judge Evans asked my view as to public opinion about the removal of Fremont (it was at the time the investigation into the charges against Fremont was going on), my answer was that it was like fried wool, greatly mixed; that when he was first appointed I thought he was the right man in the right place, but now I did not think that he or any other man at the head of the civil or military service knew the true key of the west. Judge Evans said: 'Why, don't you consider the Mississippi River the key of the west?' I told him, no, sir. He said Why? I hesitated. Judge Evans then assured me that he and Miss Carroll were agents of the Government (he has acknowledged here that he was an agent of the Government) and as a consequence I was glad to give the information where it would reach headquarters, as I had no means of going to the right parties."

Question—By Mr. McDougal. You had reported to General Grant before that?

Answer. As a pilot.

Q. Why could not you have communicated the information to General Grant at the time?

Ans. Because at the time I saw a good many reasons against it and I thought I would hold on until I knew how the cat was going to jump. I did not think he had the power, and besides I thought they were going to remove him.

Q.—By Mr. Williams. How large a command had Grant at that time?

Ans. He had about six thousand or eight thousand men. I kept the thing to myself until I had it matured. I explained the whole thing to Judge Evans, and he being partially acquainted with the topography of the country, understood it completely. He said to me, "You ought to write that down." I told him I would gladly do so but I was going away and I was not a good writer anyhow. Judge Evans said: "Miss Carroll is going to Washington to-morrow morning with dispatches, and if you will write and send it to her (handing her address in Washington) she will lay it directly before the War Department.

Q. Was this before you had ever seen Miss Carroll?

Ans. This was in conversation the first time I ever saw her. She was a little deaf and Judge Evans did most of the talking. I wrote a letter at Cairo in accordance with my promise and sent it to Miss Carroll, and about ten days afterwards I received a communication from her stating that she had received and laid it before the War Department and that they were surprised as well as pleased at the information it contained, and that if found to be correct it would be of the utmost importance. They also stated, she said, that Andy Johnson in consultation with them had stated that the Tennessee River was not navigable, and she asked me to write farther, even at the risk of repetition. I wrote and in about ten days after I received her second letter, about the 15th of December. In the meantime my opinion of General Grant had changed considerably in some respects, and in conversation with Major Gillam and John Barclay, my partner, we concluded that they were not doing justice to General Grant and that if I would give him the information it might lead to something, perhaps to a command of the expedition.

I took the papers up to his office; it was about the 15th of December, 1861. I handed him first a copy of the first letter to Miss Carroll, consisting of three sheets of foolscap; one was about the obstructions of the Mississippi, giving the reasons why they could not be overcome; the second was the advantages of the Tennessee, and the third was a general description of the country from the Tennessee River through by Chattanooga and Knoxville, also across to Memphis, also across to and down the Tombigbee River. I had keel-boated and steam-boated in all the navigable streams of the South when a boy.

Q. What did General Grant say?

Ans. He asked if I would let him have them. I told him I did not want to lose them and he promised to give them back, but he never has done so.

Q. Have you ever asked for them?

Ans. I have.

Q. What did he say?

Ans. Well, he says he has not got any letters of mine. The remainder of the story up to the close of the war is historical. I wrote letters to Miss Carroll from time to time, as she states, In 1865 I came on to Washington. My partners, who were living in the South, had sold General Pillow's certificate of valuation for cotton at a very low figure, and in 1865 we had one thousand bales of cotton in which I had one-fourth interest. I came on to Washington feeling that my services had been well worth to the government the 25 per cent. duty, intending to ask that they would relieve me of the 25 per cent. tax, and allow me to bring it in free, and that would cover my losses. I called on Judge Evans and asked him to get me a permit to bring in one thousand bales of cotton. He promised to do so, and wrote out a permit for ten thousand. I refused to accept it ; I only wanted it for one thousand bales, which was all I was entitled to.

The next day, or a day or two afterwards, a publication came out in the *National Intelligencer*, of which I knew nothing until it was shown to me. The following is a copy of the article.

[Communicated.]

CAPTAIN CHARLES M. SCOTT—PLAN OF THE TENNESSEE CAMPAIGN.

The capitulation of General Lee and the surrender of his army ends the rebellion forever as a belligerent power, and it is now in order to nominate for historic honors the individuals who have contributed an important part to this grand result.

Those who have studied the campaigns and battles of the war in their logical connections and sequences cannot fail to have perceived that the moves up the Tennessee River, in 1861, have had a more important bearing upon the termination of this struggle than any other campaign of the war. It made the opening of the Mississipi River possible, broke the Confederate power throughout its great valley, and opened the gate for the great Sherman into the South Atlantic States, enabling him to co-operate with General Grant in the siege of Petersburg and Richmond, and leaving Davis without a country in which to create another army.

In the early stages of the civil war two theories for its prosecution obtained. One was to send an expedition down the Mississippi River to unite with the blockading fleet and crush the rebellion by external pressure. This was known as the "anaconda theory." The other was to send a colum into the interior of the rebel States and pierce the heart, or, as it was sometimes said, to break the backbone of the rebellion.

The disaster at Bull Run advertised how difficult it was with the forces then available, to penetrate the enemy's country, and General Sherman, commanding in Kentucky, stated to the Secretary of War that it would require a column of at least 250,000 men to penetrate the cotton States through east Tennessee, or to make the grand expedition down the Mississippi, then preparing, a success.

On my visit to the West in the fall of 1861, I became thoroughly satisfied with the soundness of the view as expressed by General Sherman that the Mississippi expedition, if then persisted in, would prove a failure, and to succeed we must strike the vitals of the rebellion at some other point.

Three or four days after the repulse of our gunboats at Columbus and the defeat of our arms at Belmont, I sought for information an interview with Captain Charles M Scott, whose wife, a refined and educated lady, I had met in St. Louis, who informed me that her husband had long been a professional pilot on the Mississippi, and was at the wheel of the Memphis at the critical time when it brought off safely General Grant and his army from the field of Belmont.

I found Captain Scott a gentleman remarkable for his ardor and devotion to the Union, for the force and clearness of his intellect and the extent and accuracy of this information. He cited many facts going to show that it would be impossible for the gunboats, then being fitted out, to pass the batteries on the Mississippi, and stated that the true policy was to divert our gunboats up the Tennessee River where they could meet no insuperable obstructions. He suggested what seemed never to have occurred to the Government, that the Tennessee was navigable for our gunboats to the foot of the Muscle Shoals in Alabama.

Judge Evans, of Texas, was present and participated in this interview, and being also well acquained with the topography of the Southwest, fully concurred in the views expressed, and perceiving their immense bearing upon the destruction of the rebellion, suggested to me the importance of requesting them in writing for the use of the Government. On my return home I received from Captain Scott a letter fully detailing the facts I had elicited in St. Louis, from which I prepared and read about the last of November, to Col. Thomas A. Scott, then Assistant Secretary of War, the following paper :

"NOVEMBER 30, 1861.

"The civil and military authorities seem laboring under a grave mistake in regard to the true key of the war in the

Southwest. It is not the Mississippi, but the Tennessee River. It is well known that the eastern part or the farming interests of Tennessee and Kentucky are generally loyal, while the middle and western parts, or what are known as the planting districts, are in sympathy with the traitors, but except in the extreme western part the Union sentiment still lives.

"Now, all the military preparations made in the West indicate that the Mississippi River is the point to which the authorities are directing their attention. On that river many battles must be fought and heavy risks must be incurred before any impression can be made on the enemy, all of which could be avoided by using the Tennessee River. This is navigable for first-class boats to the Mississippi line, and is open to navigation all the year, while the distance is only two hundred and fifty miles by river from Paducha, on the Ohio.

"The Tennessee River offers many advantages over the Mississippi. We should avoid the almost impregnable batteries of the enemy which cannot be taken without great danger and great risk of life to our forces, from the fact that our boats, if crippled, would fall a prey to the enemy by being swept by the current to them and away from the relief of our friends. But even should we succeed, still we will only have begun the war, for we shall then have to fight to the country from whence the enemy derives his supplies. Now, to advance up the Tennessee River would avoid all this danger, for if our boats were crippled they would drop back with the current to their friends and escape all damages. But an advantage still would be a tendency to cut the enemy's lines in two by reaching the Memphis & Charleston Railroad, threatening Memphis, which lies about one hundred and fifty miles due west, and no defensible point between ; also Nashville, only ninety miles northeast, and Florence and Tuscumbia, in North Alabama, forty miles east. A movement in this direction would do more to relieve our friends in Kentucky, and inspire the loyal hearts in East Tennessee than the possession of the whole Mississippi

River. If well executed it would cause the evacuation of all those formidable fortifications on which the rebels ground their hopes of success ; and in the event of our fleet attacking Mobile, the presence of our troops in the northern part of that State would be of material benefit to the fleet. Again, the aid our forces would receive from the loyal men in Tennessee would enable them to crush the last traitor in that region, and the separation of the two extremes would do more than one hundred battles for the Union cause.

"The Tennessee River is crossed by the Memphis & Louisville Railroad and the Memphis & Nashville Railroad at Hamburg, where the river makes the big bend to the east and touches the northeast corner of Mississippi, entering the northwest corner of Alabama, forming the arc of a circle to the south, enters the State of Tennessee at the northeast of Alabama, and if it does not touch the northwest corner of Georgia comes very near it.

"It is but eight miles from Hamburg to the Memphis & Charleston Railroad, which road goes through Tuscumbia, and only two miles from the river, which it crosses at Decatur, thirty miles above, intersecting with the Nashville & Chattanooga road at Stephenson, Alabama.

"The Tennessee River never has less than three feet to Hamburg on the shoalest bar, and during the fall, winter and spring months there is always water for the largest boats that are used on the Mississippi River.

"It follows from the above that in making the Mississippi the key of the war in the West, or rather in overlooking the Tennessee River, the subject is not understood by the superiors in command."

The Assistant Secretary of War, Col. Scott, with his uncommonly acute and practical mind, saw at a flash the immense value of the paper, and desired me to leave it with him, which I did, remarking that I had gathered this information for the benefit of my country and brought it to him that he might use it for that end, if in his superior judgment he deemed it of sufficient importance.

I informed Captain Scott, of St. Louis, what action I had taken, and on the 5th of January, 1862, I received a letter from which the following is an extract:

"I assure you I felt flattered at the approval you say my views on the true key of the war in the West met with from those in high position· * * * Our gunboats are not fit to retreat against the current of the western rivers, as their principal guns are placed forward; they are not so efficient against an enemy below them. They have either to fight with their stern guns, which are but two to the boat, or else anchor by the stern and thus lose all the advantage that their motion gives them and become a target for the enemy, who will not be slow to find the range.

"If you will look at a map of the Western States you will see in what a position Buckner would be placed if we would now make a strong advance up the Tennessee. He would be compelled to fall back out of Kentucky, as if he did not this force would take Nashville in his rear and force him to lay down his arms.

"Our gunboats will be fit for service in about fifteen days at farthest."

After the expedition moved up the Tennessee River Mrs. Scott enclosed to me from time to time the following extracts from letters received from her husband.

"IN SIGHT OF FORT HENRY, ⎱
"TENNESSEE RIVER, February 4, 1862. ⎰

" I think this move is the beginning of the plan I proposed to Miss Carroll. It looks so, for I was the only man on the first three boats that arrived here who had ever been up the Tennessee River before, and we came all the way in the night without any trouble, I leading all the way. The distance from Paducha is only sixty-five miles. We are now just over the line and in Tennessee.

"FOUR MILES BELOW FORT HENRY,
"TENNESSEE RIVER, February 6, 1862.

"No other casualty but the Essex has occurred. The enemy seemed to know that she was the only boat that had her boilers on deck."

"FORT HENRY, February 7, 1862.

"I would like to have you write to Miss Carroll and tell her that I am glad to find our army on the move up the Tennessee, and hope we shall continue until we reach the State of Mississippi, when, I think, we may soon end the war.

"By taking the Memphis & Charleston railroad we shall have command of their lines of communication, menacing them at every point. This is the wedge which I think rail-splitter knows how to use to the best advantage."

"FORT HENRY, February 17, 1862.

"There is no doubt that Fort Donelson was the hardest fight ever fought on this continent. What the moral effect will be remains to be seen. * * * I think Sumner said a truth when he said slavery brutalizes man. Such acts as have been perpetrated by the Mississippi, Arkansas, Texas and Louisiana troops would be a disgrace to devils, especially the Texas and Mississippi regiments."

"FORT HENRY, March 6, 1862.

"No one knows where we are going, but I think it will be (according to what I wrote to Miss Carroll last fall) two hundred miles further up, which will have the same effect on Memphis that the move on this place had on Columbus; for if you will take a map and run your eye up the Tennessee River you will find that going up you go nearly due South until opposite Memphis, and it is a good natural road into Memphis which cannot be destroyed; also it cuts the main connection between the East and the West; this move will completely break the backbone of the Rebellion, or at least put the misery where it rightfully belongs—in the Cotton States."

"PITTSBURG LANDING, March 17, 1862.

"I have not a doubt, without being an egotist, but my suggestions through Miss Carroll were the first ever made to the administration that the Tennessee River was the best point to attack the enemy and shorten the war."

From Pittsburg Landing, March 17, 1862, Captain Scott addressed me as follows:

"Miss Carroll, I think you will find that as far as we have gone every prediction has been fulfilled, namely, that the occupation of the Tennessee would render Columbus and Memphis untenable in a military point of view, and it was our strongest point of attack. This was proven at Fort Donelson, for had our gunboats been fighting down stream they would most assuredly have been taken when they were injured."

In anticipation of the history of this civil war I deem it a pleasant duty, on this day of the nation's rejoicing, to make known to the American people how much they are indebted to Captain Charles M. Scott for the crowning victory which now thrills with joy every patriot, for when the history shall be correctly written it will be obliged to treat the campaign up the Tennessee River as the turning point which decided the triumph of the Union over treason and rebellion, and that this campaign was the result of the information herewith submitted was fully confirmed by confirmation of the Hon. Thomas A. Scott, Assistant Secretary of War, the last of May, 1862, to whom the country is incalculably indebted for inaugurating the movement.   ANNA ELLA CARROLL.

MARYLAND, April 10, 1865.

"LIBRARY OF CONGRESS, }
"WASHINGTON, June 27, 1865. }

"I hereby certify that the foregoing is a true copy of the original communication, signed, Anna Ella Carroll, published in the *National Intelligencer* of April 12, 1865, on file in the Library of Congress.

"Witness my hand and the seal of my office the day and year above written. A. R. SPOFFORD,

Librarian of Congress."

Q.—By Mr. McDougal. Were you the author of this letter of the 23d of May, 1864? ⟵———

Ans. Yes, sir.

The letter was put in evidence as follows.

" *To the Editor of Tribune:*

Sir, an article appeared in your columns recently calling attention to the claim of a Miss Carroll for originating the plan of the Tennessee campaign, and as I do not believe that you would do an injustice to any one or lend your columns to assist a fraud or further an unjust claim, I beg leave to say that I claim to have originated in November, 1861, in a letter sent by me to the Secretary of War, dated 18th of November, 1861, and directed to the care of Miss Carroll, as she represented herself to me as a secret agent sent out by the Government to collect information, and I was assured by those accompanying her that such was the fact. She has since published my letter to the Secretary of War, simply changing the address as her own production, and thinking I am out of the way, she has the effrontery to claim remuneration for it.

I have never made any claim for remuneration for doing what I believed to be my duty, although I lost by doing so. Many lost their lives in the same cause, so I felt remunerated when my humble services were beneficial to it.

What I did is known to the commanding officers that I served under, and I can refer with pride to him that the nation has honored with its highest gift, also to Admiral S. P. Lee and Captain Frank Ramsey, of the Navy, who will each testify that I did my whole duty in whatever position I was placed. But while I make no claim for doing my duty, I do make a distinct claim for an invention that enabled the Government to carry on the war in the West at a great deal less cost than it could have done without such invention, viz, the shield to protect pilots from the enemy's riflemen stationed along the shores, and also the invention of the signal system in use on our western rivers, that is acknowledged to have done more to save life and property than anything since the invention of steam, and I shall present a distinct claim for remuneration for these two inventions at an early date.　　　　CHARLES M. SCOTT.

ST. LOUIS, Mo., May 23, 1874.

Miss Carroll began to soft soap me and told me that the object in publishing that article was to manufacture public opinion for me, and that she and Judge Evans would put a claim to Congress in my name and engineer it through and I would divide with them. That was the statement to me. I refused in toto. I told them I had only done my duty and all I asked was the privilege of bringing in my cotton, so that thing dropped right there. A year or two afterwards I saw in the newspapers about Miss Carroll's claim.

Q.—By Mr. Williams. What became of your cotton claim? Did you get it through?

*Ans. No sir, I did not. The very day of the death of Lincoln I presented my papers and stated what they were. He said he would look them over. I told him that I had been

---

* I had tried in vain to get to see Lincoln and had got out of money and was preparing to leave Washington by the next train, when, passing Willard's Hotel, I saw General Rawlins standing at the door, and stepped up to him and shook hands. He asked me if I had succeeded. I told him no. He then asked me if I had seen the General (Grant, he meant). I answered, no, I did not know he was in the city. He said yes, and asking me to accompany him, we went into the parlor of the hotel and found Grant sitting there, surrounded by a number of strangers. General Rawlins presented me to Grant, who shook hands with me and asked me if I had succeeded in seeing the President. I told him no, and had given up, as I could not afford to stay any longer, being out of money. Grant, turning to the gentlemen he had been talking to, excused himself for a few moments, and asking me to accompany him went through the Treasury building (the shortest way to the White House) and over to the White House and up stairs to the President's office. All made way for him and at the door of the office, when Grant's name was announced, the door flew open and Grant, taking me by the hand, introduced me to Lincoln as a loyal man and

there nearly a month trying to get them through and was completely out of money. He told me that it would make no difference, that he would look over the papers and send them to me in St. Louis if they were correct. I started from here (Washington) about five o'clock in the evening, and at Harrisburg, next morning, I heard of his death. My papers disappeared. I heard nothing more of them and there was no use of coming on and prosecuting the claim without the papers. I saw this publication of Miss Carroll's claim and I wrote to her about it and the matter dropped for the time. The next thing I saw was her pamphlet. I wrote to her denouncing it as a fraud and stating that I should make a claim myself and expose it, as I considered it a fraud. I stated in my letter to her that she had published my first letter almost verbatim in her pamphlet. As published in the pamphlet it corresponds with the publication in the *Intelligencer* article, but she gives it as my letter in the *Intelligencer* while in the pamphlet she gives the same letter as her own. The thing stopped at the time. Again I heard there was a claim and I wrote to Mr. Stone, in the House here, about a year ago (1875), telling him where he could find the documents and this *Intelligencer* article and denouncing the claim as a fraud. I stated that it was not Miss Carroll that the claim was for, that she was merely a stalking horse and Judge Evans was the real claimant. That ended it at the time and I supposed it was the end of it altogether. When I came on here this winter at the request of some steamboat men to explain a Steamboat Bill, I found that

---

his friend, who had rendered important services to the Government, and would be pleased if the President would listen to my story, and if he considered the request I had to make proper, he would take it as a favor to have it granted. He then excused himself and retired. I then stated my case to Lincoln and asked for a permit to bring in 1,000 bales of cotton free of the twenty-five per cent. duty levied on cotton, and presented my papers to Lincoln, who took them and told me he would look over them and if they were all right I should have the permit. I told him I had spent all my money and could not afford to stop any longer.

Miss Carroll had her claim up again, and I thought if it was going on so the only way was to put in my claim and let the thing come squarely up on its merits. I have here some papers that I want to put in, Major Gillam's letter and John Barclay's letter. They are as follows, and also a communication cut from the Cincinnati *Commercial* and forwarded to me :

First, "Personally appeared before me, L. S. Brotherton, a Notary Public in and for the County of Saint Louis and State of Missouri, John Barclay, a resident of Saint Clair, in the State of Illinois, who on oath states :

'On or about the 17th day of November, 1861, I went on the steamboat Belle Memphis as pilot, she being engaged as a Government transport.

I furthermore testify that on the arrival of the boat at Cairo my partner on the boat, Charles M. Scott (pilot) consulted me as to the propriety of his sending to a Miss Carroll, at Washington City, certain information for the use of the Government. My memory is that I told Scott that he ought by all means to do so. He appeared somewhat undecided which was best, to send it to her and through her to the hands of the Government, or to give it direct to the commander at Cairo (General Grant). My understanding afterwards was that he transmitted his papers to Miss Carroll as above indicated. On or about the 19th of November, 1861, Mr. Scott read to me from papers prepared by him a full description of first, the difficulties to be met by going down the Mississippi River with an army, as he suggested, of even a million of men, whereas my decision was that all the armies in the country could not go down that way ; secondly, he gave a description of the Tennessee as the true point of attact with a synopsis of the advantages to be gained by our forces taking it. Previous to this I had heard no suggestion of any attempt by way of the Tennessee River, but knowing that Mr. Scott, from his early boating experience on that stream, had a perfect knowledge of it and of its importance, I had confidence in his judgment. The engrossing topic in the way of attacking the enemy at this time being the Mississippi River. I am satisfied that the plan of the Tennessee campaign was sent to Miss Carroll in November, for I saw her letter responsive thereto. On or about the 15th of December of the same year Mr. Scott showed me a letter from Miss Carroll in which she stated to him that every statement he had made was verified in the Surveyor General's office, and that the movement up the Tennessee was to be carried out.

Mr. Scott and myself consulted at length as to the propriety of showing the whole correspondence to General Grant, who was at that time commander at Cairo. He (Scott) thought it was right that General Grant should know of the contemplated movement so as to enable him (the General) to secure a command in it, and I warmly advised him to do so.

Then Mr. Scott took the correspondence and plan and said he was going to lay the whole matter before the General, and on his return, late that night, told me he had done so.

And now I am convinced as I have ever felt, that to my partner, Mr. Scott, is due the originating of the campaign up the Tennessee.'   JOHN BARCLAY.

Subscribed and sworn to before me this 8th of November, 1874."   L. S. BROTHERTON.

Notary Public, Saint Louis County, Missouri.

" MAJOR GILLAM'S STATEMENT.

I was Major of the Twenty-Eighth Illinois Volunteers; I was stationed at Fort Holt in Kentucky, opposite Cairo. Ill., during the months of October, November and December, 1861. I frequently met Captain Charles M. Scott, and having been acquainted with him previously, we had frequent conversations in regard to the movements to be made to suppress the rebellion. At that time it was the general opinion that we were going down the Mississippi River. Mr. Scott strenuously opposed it in our conversations and emphatically declared we could not go down the Mississippi with a million of men if the different defensible points were defended by 15,000 resolute men to each point, but by advancing up the Tennessee River we would either force the evacuation or surrender of every defensible position on the Mississippi, as far south as we could go up the Tennessee; this included Memphis and all above Randolph, Fort Pillow, Island No. 10 and Columbus. He also pointed out that with the gunboats to keep the river open below and with our army well secured on the river as close to Corinth as possible, and breaking the railroad we would not only secure the Mississippi but seriously threaten Mobile and Montgomery by the Tombigbee and Alabama rivers on the south, Nashville on the north and assist the loyal men of East Tennessee.

Scott also claimed that there was always as much average depth of water in the Tennessee to Big Bend Shoals as there was in the Ohio, and that it had the further advantage of not being obstructed by ice in winter.

About the middle of November, 1861, Scott read to me a long communication embodying his views with a description of the obstacles to be encountered by going down the Mississippi as well as those of the Tennessee, and the character of the country lying between and up to Chattanooga, also down to Mobile, all of which Scott claimed to have been over several times and which from my own observations and information from others I have since found to be correct. This information Scott informed me he was going to forward to the War Department. In about ten or twelve days after this conversation, Scott showed me a letter from Washington, in which it was stated that his communication had been received and laid before Scott, the Assistant Secretary of War (Tom Scott), and that he was surprised as well as pleased at the information it contained, which, if found to be correct, would be of the utmost importance to the Government, but that Andy Johnson had given it as his opinion that the Tennessee was not navigable. The letter also requested Captain Scott to write again such further information and that it would be laid before the War Department at once.

About the 15th of December, 1861, I met Captain Scott, and he showed me another letter from Washington, in which it was stated that the information that he furnished had been found to be correct, and that the movement up the Tennessee was resolved on. Scott consulted with me as to showing this information to Grant, as he thought that justice had not been shown Grant in respect to the Belmont affair, and he thought that by furnishing him (Grant) this information it would enable him to get command of the expedition. I counseled him to do it, and the next time we met he told me he had done so. I found that every statement made to me by Captain Scott, was correct as far as related to the Tennessee, and I believe that the United States Government is more indebted to him for the victories that followed our advance up the Tennessee than any other human being, and hope that even at this late day justice may be done him for services that in their results were second to none rendered by any other.

Respectfully,
BARCLAY C. GILLAM."

Subscribed and sworn to before me this 22d day of June, A. D. 1876.　　　　　　　　EPHRAIM J. PEMBERTON,

County Judge Schuyler County, Illinois.

"ST. LOUIS.

To MISS CARROLL:—Respected Miss, your pamphlet came to hand to-day, and I assure you that. I was very much surprised when I read it to find that I am ignored altogether in the authorship of the Tennessee campaign and Miss Carroll alone is the author of the plan. I would respectfully ask of you if this is justice to me. I have asked no pecuniary reward from either the Government or any one else, but I cannot sit quiet and have the product of my brain awarded to another without making a protest against it. I may have allowed Colonel Badeau in his life of General Grant to credit Grant indirectly with being the author, but I think the time has come when I should claim what I believe is justly my due, viz: the credit of originating the Tennessee campaign. In your pamphlet, page 11, you quote my first letter verbatim as your own, and on page 15 after distinctly claiming, you again quote my letter from before Vicksburg. Now, in conclusion, I beg leave to notify you that if this claim is not withdrawn, I shall take means to explode it. With respect I subscribe myself,

Your obedient servant,

CHARLES M. SCOTT.

To Miss A. E. Carroll, Washington City."

Question.—By Mr. McDougal. You have stated that when Judge Evans wrote that permit for you for that cotton he made it 10,000 bales.

Answer.—Yes sir.

Ques.—Did he hand it to you to sign without reading it to you.

Ans.—He handed the paper to me all ready to sign. He did not read to me but handed to me to read.

Ques.—And you read it and saw that it was for 10,000 bales.

Ans.—Yes sir.

Ques.—What was your precise language in regard to that.

Ans.— I said this is wrong; I have no claim for 10,000 bales. I told him I had no right to it.

Ques.—What did he say.

Ans.—He said you might as well take it, that everybody else was doing so, and he proposed that I should give him an interest in it.

Ques.—What interest did he propose you should give him.

Ans.—I have now forgotten the exact amount.

Ques.—State the precise language that he used.

Ans.—I cannot now state the precise amount that he proposed I should give him.

Ques.—But he made a definite proposition to you to share a portion of it.

Ans.—Yes sir, a definite proposition.

Ques.—By Mr. Williams. One-half or one-third, or so much as that?

Ans.—I think I was to give him and Miss Carroll an equal half of it; an equal half of all I got through over my thousand bales. That is as near as I can recollect it now.

Ques.—Was Miss Carroll present at the time?

Ans.—She was there; it was down on F street, I think.

Ques.—What did she say in relation to it?

Ans.—Nothing. She very seldom did any talking; Judge Evans did all the talking between us.

Ques.—By Mr. Williams. Could she understand your conversation?

Ans.—Most of it; Judge Evans would frequently have to speak pretty loud to her.

Ques.—Was there any loud talking between her and Judge Evans in relation to the cotton?

Ans.—No; he stated my objections to her rather loud.

Ques.—What did she say in reply to your objections?

Ans.—I do not recollect now because my mind was so uneasy about other things. I recollect that I definitely rejected it; that is the principal point.

Ques.—In what way did you acquire this knowledge of the navigation of the Tennessee River and of the country that lay between the Tennessee and the Mississippi?

Ans.—When I was a boy of thirteen, I was a cook on a keel-boat and I keel-boated on that river and the Tombigbee river, and in the season when the Tennessee would rise, I would float down on the cotton-boats landing here and there and lying wind-bound for days and in that way I acquired a knowledge of the different points on the Mississippi. Then frequently we would come up the river on a Louisville or St. Louis boat to Memphis and walk across to Eastport or Waterloo. I had also experience in keel-boating up the Tombigbee river and those other streams in that country, and frequently about the close of the season a big crew of us would come up to Cottongin port or wherever the trip might end and a large portion would get paid off and walk across through the Indian country to Eastport; it was Waterloo then; I hunted over nearly every foot of the country when I was a boy; I also served ten months under Sam Houston in the Texas war and acquired some little knowledge of military tactics and I applied the one knowledge to the other and originated the idea of the Tennessee campaign or the idea of it from that knowledge.

Ques.—What information had you about the fortification upon the Mississippi River?

Ans.—I came up the river in June, 1861; I took a good view of it then as I passed along in front and knowing the country around I was pretty well aware that I could not get by them.

Ques.—Had you been a keel-boatman on the Tennessee?

Ans.—I had.

Ques.—Then you knew the depth of water in the Tennessee?

Ans.—I did, from the shoals to the mouth. From the mouth to Chattanooga, I was on the first steamboat that ever went over Mussel Shoals, laying the warps for her in 1831 and helping to remove the Cherokees under Gen. Scott in 1838; I was mate of the same boat; we brought them from Fort Cass opposite Calhoun on the Tennessee river.

Ques.—By Mr. Evans. In that conversation between us did not I interrogate you particularly in regard to the points on the Tennessee river, as to whether the gunboats could go over the Mussel Shoals, and did I not also interrogate you with regard to the depth of water in Mobile bay?

Ans.—You did.

Ques.—And as to the probability of being able to move up the Alabama and Tombigbee rivers?

Ans.—No sir; nothing that I understood so at all; I suggested the idea of striking the Tombigbee river from Eastport and using it for transportation down and attacking Mobile from the north.

Q.—Did I not call your attention to that?

Ans.—Not at all.

Ques.—And as to the probability of Farragut's fleet passing Dog River bar?

Ans.—No sir; I have no knowledge of such a thing, because Farragut's fleet was not known at that time.

Ques.—By Mr. Williams. In 1861?

Ans.—In 1861 it was not known as attacking New Orleans or engaged down in that country that I heard of.

Ques.—By Mr. McDougal. Did Mr. Evans question you as to the probability of any fleet being able to pass Dog River bar?

Ans.—No sir.

Ques.—By Mr. Williams. In this conversation with Mr. Evans and Miss Carroll at St. Louis, did you understand that she was to act as your agent in presenting to the War Department your views in regard to the Tennessee river?

Ans.—Yes, sir.

Ques.—And not that you were to furnish her information that she was to use on her own account?

Ans.—I understood that the information was to be laid before the War Department directly from me; I had no idea of doing anything but my duty in the matter and I was willing to give it to the devil to carry if I could get him to carry it to the right place.

Ques.—How many pilots were there on the river that were loyal?

Ans.—Out of 148 St. Louis pilots that ran south only five.

Ques.—By Mr. McDougal. Where were you born?

Ans. In Ireland.

Ques. How old were you when you came to this country.

Ans.—About three years old.

CHARLES M. SCOTT.

The witness submitted in evidence the following letters :

HEADQUARTERS ARMIES OF THE UNITED STATES, }
CITY POINT, VA., March 18, 1865. }

CAPTAIN:—I was placed in a position in September, 1861, where I could see the course pursued by you at that stage of the rebellion. It was my understanding that you had been an old Mississippi river pilot and had left the Lower Mississippi, about the last chance that was left to escape. I know nothing about your personal sacrifices further than you have stated them to me, but have no reason to doubt those statements. It gives me pleasure to say that at a time when the great majority of your profession were decidedly disloyal, or at least sympathized with the rebellion, you professed the strongest devotion to the old Union and, as long as I remained in command at Cairo, stood always ready to conduct either transports or armed vessels wherever Government authorities wished them to be taken. You also furnished information of the Mississippi and its defences and of the Cumberland, which proved both correct and valuable.

Yours truly,   U. S. GRANT,
Lieutenant-General.

To Charles M. Scott, Mississippi River pilot.

PITTSBURG LANDING, April 15, 1862.

This is to certify that Charles M. Scott, a pilot on the Mississippi river, has been in Government service and detained on the Cumberland and Tennessee rivers until the present time, thereby preventing him from appearing for examination before the local inspectors of St. Louis at the time required.

I will further state that Captain Scott, from his great knowledge of the Tennessee and Mississippi rivers and the interest felt by him in the Union cause, has been able to give valuable information from time to time and has done so cheerfully.

U. S. GRANT,
Major General.

To the Board of Inspectors St. Louis, Missouri.

MISSISSIPPI SQUADRON, FLAGSHIP BLACK HAWK, } MOUND CITY. March 1, 1865. }

SIR:—I accept to take effect at the expiration of your leave on the 31st inst., with much regret your resignation as a first-class pilot in this Squadron. But I cannot withhold my acceptance in view of the state of your health, the long, able and willing public service you have rendered in the army and navy from the outbreak of the rebellion and because you have provided not one but several substitutes who are qualified pilots. When you wish to return to the service you will be gladly reappointed. With my thanks for your good example and wishes for your health and happiness, I have the honor to be Sir,   Your obedient servant,

S. P. LEE,

Acting Rear Admiral Commanding Mississippi Squadron.

To Charles M. Scott, First-class Pilot.

The following communication was published in the *Cincinnati Commercial* and was sent by the author with whom I was stopping in Ohio:

COMMUNICATED.

"General Buell again. Who planned the campaign in the West?

EDITORS COMMERCIAL:—A writer in your issue of the 22d, claims that it was the scintillation of General Buell's military genius which enlightened the War Department on the plan of operations which opened the Tennessee and Cumberland rivers, which involved the capture of Forts Henry and Donelson, causing the immediate evacuation of Bowling Green, etc., and that Generals Grant, Pope and Halleck are all greatly indebted to that splendid genius for their elevation to high military honors. A very modest assumption, truly, considering how General Buell has carried out his programme.

Now, Sirs, a friend of mine, a pilot on the Mississippi, Tennessee and Cumberland, of over thirty years experience, and who understood those rivers like a book, and who escaped from Memphis and reaching Cairo through Missouri, passed the month of August, 1861 in my family. During this time we had several conversations on the plan of the Southwestern campaign. He showed conclusively and laid almost precisely the plan of the campaign as it has been carried out. He had an interview with General Prentiss while commandant at Cairo, convincing him of the impracticability of successfully attacking the rebels by the way of the Mississippi, and that the only feasible route was up the Cumberland and Tennessee, and I think expressed the same views to Fremont.

The following extract from a strictly private letter will show that the War Department was informed by him of the feasibility before General Buell was even appointed to the command of the Army of the Ohio He says:

Immediately after the Belmont affair, I met a Government Agent from Washington, who was in St. Louis for the purpose of enquiring into the public sentiment in regard to the removal of Fremont, and to obtain such other useful information as would be beneficial to the Government. He was referred to me for a knowledge of the river, when after he had shown me his letters of recommendation, I gave him all the information in my power. After I had satisfied him about the river he asked me the state of feeling in regard to Fremont. I told him it was divided. For myself I believed I was deceived in him, as I did not think he understood the true key of the West, nor did I believe any of our civil or military leaders understood it. On enquiring what I meant, I took a map and after showing the difficulties and dangers of an advance down the Mississippi, and how little was to be gained by it, I then explained the advantage of an advance up the Tennessee into the heart of Rebeldom, and by cutting their lines of communication, render their forces unavailable at more than one point. As I was on the point of starting to Cairo, he requested me to commit my views to writing and to forward them to his address in Washington, to be laid before the Secretary of War. This I did, and shortly after received a letter acknowledging its receipt and stating that my views had been submitted to the head of the War Department and they were astonished as well as pleased at the information it contained which if found correct, would be of much importance to the Government; that means would be taken to verify it from other sources, and that any additional information I could render would be acceptable.

The battle of Belmont was fought on the 6th or 8th of November; General Buell took command about the 20th, and in a few weeks suggested to the President, to General McClellan, and to General Halleck that plan of operations which ended in smoke.

I think another individual was ahead of him in enlightening the War Department on the plan of operations. But how was it carried out? The only redeeming feature was at Pittsburg Landing, and that would have failed but for the gunboats. The usual dilly-dally which has marked all of Buell's movements had well nigh sacrificed the whole of Grant's army.

With an army of six divisions and twenty-four batteries and seven regiments of cavalry, containing in the whole not less than seventy thousand men, he did less than General Mitchell with fifteen thousand; let the rebels concentrate an army almost within striking distance and never made an attempt to disturb them. He frittered away the whole glorious summer doing nothing, making himself the sport and contempt of his army; till it passed into a by-word that where Buell was there was no danger. But let us follow him in his chase back to Louisville and see what can be said of Mumfordsville, since your correspondent has become his apologist for that disgraceful affair, and with what energy he pursued Bragg from Green River. I avail myself of another correspondent who was on the spot and had opportunities of observation equal to J. L.

A large portion of Buell's army entered Bowling Green on

the 11th of September and remained till the 15th, and Mumfordsville was taken on the 16th. I quote: And here, in my opinion, the blunders, mistake or treachery of Buell began. Instead of keeping his divisions, which were consolidated, on the road, he massed them in one tremenduous camp and commenced fortifying as if the rebels were going to attack us in one of the strongest positions in the world. Here we lay and Bragg sending a small force from Glasgow to attract our attention, pushed on with his main force and gained time to make his successful descent upon Colonel Wilder and his gallant band at Green River bridge. I am confident that had we left Bowling Green twenty-four hours earlier to our cause might have been averted, and probably Bragg's ^entire plan of invading Kentucky frustrated. On Monday evening the 15th we crossed Barren River, and towarns evening of the 16th left the pike and started out to the right towards Glasgow. The road was narrow and rough; the equinoxial storm came on, we camped in the open fields; the wagons could not come up and we had neither supper or blankets.. On the 17th we drew three days rations but had no time to cook them and started at 1 P. M. and marched until 11 P. M. We were in fine spirits when we received orders to march again in two hours, as all confidently expected a battle on the morrow; but Buell, our evil genius, was present and the sun was gilding the western hills as we marched with colors flying but in complete silence past the headquarters of the General commanding. He was invisible as usual, and we got not even a look, much less an encouraging cheering word. If it had been Mitchell we should not have gone by that way was the word passed along the line of Old Starry's boys. Another thing which served to discourage us at the same time that it angered us was meeting the paroled prisoners who had been compelled to surrender to overwhelming numbers at the bridge the day before. These noble men need no eulogy, their acts speak for them more eloquently than any words can do, and that defense will be marked in future history as one of the noblest of the war. But where will stand the name and fame of the man, who, with his impatient thousands, lay idle and made not the slightest effort to rescue them. In the varying fortunes of war some brilliant success may retrieve the name of General Buell from the reproach of treason, but it can never remove the responsibility and disgrace of that surrender from his own shoulders; but I wander. We marched six miles to a little village and cross road, our division occupying the extreme right, when our regiment was sent in advance throwing out skirmishers and the whole division deployed in line of battle. All were eager and hopeful and in condition to make a gallant fight. About 10 o'clock skirmishing began on the right and soon after on the left continuing at intervals all day. The cavalry were flying around in the road and about noon brought in quite a squad of prisoners, who reported the enemy crossing Green River. Still we considered an attack certain and rested easy thinking the delay was occasioned by the other divisions getting into position. One, two, three came and passed and still there came no order to advance. We were getting hungry. Bragg held our cracker line and we had to go to the cornfields. The night passed quietly and again in the morning we thought we would certainly move, but hour after hour passed till 10 o'clock when we were relieved by the tenth and marched to the rear. Saturday came and passed and on Sunday rumors arrived that the rebels had escaped us again. At 5 P. M. we started for Green River with the assurance that there was no one there. Bragg and his army had got three days start on the road to Louisville. We marched twelve miles and when the sun got hot the next morning moved into the woods and lay till 3 P. M., when we moved again and then back again. Tuesday morning we marched nine miles and overtook McCook's division, when we cooked lunch and started again marching sixteen miles to Nolin Creek. Wednesday we marched to Elizabethtown and got dinner and on the afternoon

made fourteen miles. Long ere this we had become satisfied
that the rebels had left the pike, and that we were to make no
immediate effort to overtake them. We were fast becoming
worn out and the excitement of pursuit being removed the men
began to straggle and the road was lined with them from No-
lens Creek to this place (Louisville). We entered the city
just at daylight on Friday, the 25th, having been thirty-two
days coming from Huntsville, a distance of three hundred and
fifty miles. So Buell's great southern campaign is ended and
we are to-day just where we were ten months ago. Our splendid army has done wonders and accomplished nothing--
marched up the hill and then down again. Surely the nation
ought to follow the journal, throw up hats and cry, great is
Buell. The feeling in the army is very bitter against him and
we believe he will never fight a battle until forced by the enemy.

From the foregoing I think three conclusions are deduci-
ble. First, Bragg fooled Buell at Bowling Green and secured
plenty of time to capture Colonel Wilder and his five thousand
men. Second, that he did the same at Green River and third,
that having three days start of Buell, he did not precipitately
(according to J. L) get out of Buell's way. And we all know
that the same strategy was again successfully played against
Buell at Perrysville.

If these trials of a conservative General will not satisfy J.
L., they have at least satisfied many who have dearest friends
in the army of the incompetence of General Buell to successfully manage it, and we rejoice that a conservative President
is at last getting sick of conservative generals, who have done
nothing but waste away the finest armies in the world, and is
putting live men in their places. For eighteen months con-
servatism has had its way and what has it accomplished; almost nothing. Let its opposite have at least a fair trial.

G. M.

Westerville, Ohio, November 24, 1862.

The occasion of this publication is as follows : I stopped at the house of Mr. McQuirk in Ohio during July and August of 1861. He had two sons in the army already and was an enthusiastic Union man. He and I had frequent talks about the war and the best points of attack and I unfolded my views to him.

The witness also submitted a copy of a letter written by Miss Carroll, protesting againt the statement contained in her pamphlet as follows :

RESPECTED MISS:—Your pamphlet came to hand to-day, and I assure you that I was very much surprised when I read it to find that I am ignored altogether in the authorship of the Tennessee Campaign, and Miss Carroll alone is the author of the plan. I would respectfully ask of you if this is justice to me. I have asked no pecuniary reward from either the Government or anyone else; but I cannot sit quiet and have the product of my brain awarded to another without making a protest against it.

I may have allowed Colonel Badeau in his life of Grant to credit Grant indirectly with being the author, but I think that the time has come when I should claim what I believe is justly due me, viz: the credit of originating the Tennessee Campaign.

In your pamphlet page 11, you quote my first letter to you verbatim as your own, and on page 15 after distinctly claiming, you again quote my letter from before Vicksburg. Now, in conclusion, I beg leave to notify you that if this claim is not withdrawn, I shall take means to explode it

With respect I subscribe myself your obed'ent servant,

CHARLES M. SCOTT.

To Miss A. E. Cornell.

In conclusion I deem it a duty I owe to myself to publish the accompanying petition, which was gotten up by my steamboat friends of St. Louis and signed by ninety-five names of steamboatmen and forwarded to the Hon. Martin S. Clavely during his first term in Congress, and of which I had no knowledge until a copy of the bill was sent to me. The petition having been read and referred to a committee where it died a natural death. I only refer to it to show the standing in which I have been held.

Very respectfully,
CHARLES M. SCOTT.

To the Senate and House of Representatives in Congress assembled:

We, your petitioners, having knowledge of the fact that Mr. CHARLES M. SCOTT has rendered valuable service to the United States Government:

1st.—In that he was the originator of the "signal system," as adopted and engrafted into the laws governing pilots on vessels in meeting or passing each other on the Mississippi River.

2d.—In that he was the originator of the "*BOILER IRON PROTECTOR*," for pilots, during the war for the "*Union*," said "protectors" rendering the pilot-house the safest place on the boat while under fire from the enemy; (many of your petitioners have taken refuge behind the "Boiler Iron" and felt *it was good to be there*.)

3d.—In that he gave valuable information to those in charge of the "Tennessee Campaign," as we have no doubt men eminent in authority at that time will now testify.

4th.—In that he was a bold, defiant and unflinching "Union man," under circumstances that thoroughly tested him (many of your petitioners fought on the other side and know whereof they speak), and it is in view of these unrewarded services and the age and condition of MR. SCOTT, that we, your petitioners, earnestly appeal to you, the representatives of the whole people, to see that this worthy servant is promptly remunerated for his valuable services to the Government. The aid he should have immediately as he in need of it now.

Time and circumstances have wrought a union in MR. SCOTT's life of that " ill-matched pair," "age and want;" his "sands of life are almost run." Will the people of this country see him depart *unrewarded, unpaid?* We hope not. They certainly will not repudiate this small but important part of the " National Debt."

And therefore we earnestly pray your honorable body will give this petition the prompt attention its importance demands, and vote MR. CHARLES M. SCOTT a sufficient sum, either in pension or otherwise, to enable him to live comfortably the few remaining days he may be spared in this life.

www.ingramcontent.com/pod-product-compliance
Lightning Source LLC
Chambersburg PA
CBHW032142080426
42733CB00008B/1174